RELIGIOUS CRISES IN MODERN AMERICA

by

Martin E. Marty

66672

The Third

Charles Edmondson Historical Lectures

Baylor University
Waco, Texas

December 2 and 3, 1980

This volume is the thirteenth volume published by the Markham Press Fund of Baylor University Press, established in memory of Dr. L. N. and Princess Finch Markham of Longview, Texas, by their daughters, Mrs. R. Matt Dawson of Waco, Texas, and Mrs. B. Reid Clanton of Longview, Texas.

The Charles Edmondson Historical Lecture Series, Number 3.

Rufus B. Spain, general editor

Publication of this series of lectures is made possible by a special grant from Dr. E. Bud Edmondson of Longview, Texas.

Library of Congress Catalog Card Number 81-80740
International Standard Book Number: 0-918954-26-6

Printed in the United States of America by the Baylor University Press, Waco, Texas 76798.

This book was set in Melior, and was printed and bound by Baylor University Press.

FOREWORD

The CHARLES EDMONDSON HISTORICAL LECTURES are made possible by an endowment fund established in 1975 by Dr. E. Bud Edmondson of Longview, Texas, in honor of his father, Mr. Charles S. B. Edmondson. The proceeds from the fund are to be used to bring to the University community outstanding historians who can interpret and communicate the events of history in such a way as to make the past meaningful to the present.

Dr. Martin E. Marty, the third Edmondson Lecturer, focuses on two religious phenomena in American history in the last hundred years, modernism and fundamentalism. These lectures can be read as sequels to the first lectures in the series by Paul K. Conkin on two earlier crises in American Christianity, religious rationalism and Darwinism.

* * * * * * * * * *

The views expressed in these lectures are those of the author and do not necessarily reflect the position of Baylor University or of the Markham Press Fund.

THE MODERNIST ATTRACTION, 1880-1925*

How can we speak of modernism and fundamentalism as crises? Given the twentieth-century record of two World Wars, a cold war, a depression, and numerous panics, by what sense of scale does one mark two theological movements as crises? What

---

*These lectures reflect the author's research into turn-of-the-century American religious changes. The documentation for these theses and comments awaits publication (in from two to four years) of a major book on the subject by the University of Chicago Press. These essays reflect the sometimes informal oral style and, of course, do not commend themselves to the footnoted approach. Readers who wish to pursue historical detail will find pioneering and reliable work in a number of volumes:

On modernism, the standard work is William R. Hutchison, *The Modernist Impulse in American Protestantism* (Cambridge, Mass.: Harvard University Press, 1976). A number of works take up milder forms of Protestant liberalism, among them Lloyd J. Averill, *American Theology in the Liberal Tradition* (Philadelphia: Westminster Press, 1967); Paul A. Carter, *The Spiritual Crisis of the Gilded Age* (Dekalb: Northern Illinois University Press, 1971); Kenneth Cauthen, *The Impact of American Religious Liberalism* (New York: Harper and Row, 1962); Frank Hugh Foster, *The Modern Movement in American Theology* (New York: Fleming H. Revell, 1939); Henry F. May, *The End of American Innocence* (Chicago: Quadrangle Books, 1964); these will lead readers to the primary sources, many of which are cited in Hutchison's bibliography.

A new standard for fundamentalism is George M. Marsden, *Fundamentalism and American Culture: The Shaping of Twentieth-Century Evangelicalism 1870-1925* (New York: Oxford University Press, 1980). Theodore Dwight Bozeman discusses the Baconian ideal in *Protestants in an Age of Science* (Chapel Hill: University of North Carolina Press, 1977); Ernest R. Sandeen points to a fusion of Princeton theology and premillennialism in *The Roots of Fundamentalism* (Chicago: University of Chicago Press, 1970); Timothy P. Weber comments on premillennialism in *Living in the Shadow of the Second Coming* (New York: Oxford University Press, 1979); James Barr provides a British critique of theology in *Fundamentalism* (Philadelphia: Westminster Press, 1978).

My description of modernity roughly parallels a popular condensation of the literature in the introduction to John Murray Cuddihy, *The Ordeal of Civility* (New York: Basic Books, 1974). Revisionist history of the evangelical reception of evolution is in James R. Moore, *The Post-Darwinian Controversies* (New York: Cambridge University Press, 1979). On tribalism, see Harold R. Isaacs, *Idols of the Tribe* (New York: Harper and Row, 1975).

None of these authors should be held responsible for what use I have made of their findings, and I have basic disagreements with many of them, but we are, as it were, walking on the same soil and readers who consult them will find it possible to satisfy their curiosity about many historical details for which two brief lectures allow no room.—M.E.M.

about the drouth and the dust bowl, tornadoes and floods—do not these produce greater upheavals? These are valid and understandable questions, but the historian of culture and religion also asks for equal time to deal with more subtle tumults of spirit. José Ortega y Gasset has said that the great changes in history occur not simply because of war and certainly not because of earthquake or cataclysm, but because the sensitive crown of the human heart tilts ever so slightly—as, for example, from hope to despair, or vice versa. So we learn to watch for processes as well as events, trends of thought as well as the sound of armor.

One can speak of a crisis that tilts the crown of the heart without being specific about religion. Yet, again, the historian of culture who is concerned with the *mentalité* of a people is likely to be watching at the side of Paul Tillich, who repeatedly urged citizenries to notice that religion is the soul of culture and culture the form of religion. So modernism and fundamentalism, while they took shape in the sphere of religion and even in the institutional embodiments, the churches, were not movements segregated into the category of "ecclesiastical history." They both were produced in response to external change and in turn produced a ripple effect far out into the public and humanist cultures. Then as now it was possible for many to ignore it serenely, but they did and do so at the expense of understanding many of the animating and depressing motions of the American spirit.

The crisis as I shall be defining it at least implicitly in these two lectures issued from the fact that modernism and fundamentalism led serious Americans to what we might call a "tyranny of limited alternatives" or, if one wishes to import a theological judgment, a tyranny of false alternatives. Thus, latecomers to the American public culture, Roman Catholics and Lutherans and the like, were learning their way around linguistically at the height of the clash between fundamentalism and modernism and then as well as ever after have acted as if these two modern inventions represented all the alternatives Christianity had ever displayed.

In undertaking this task of definition and examination, I am aware of at least four hazards, and I am also aware that there are others of which I cannot be aware. Let me point to these risks.

First, to detail these "narrowed alternatives" is to risk offending people who hold to them, citizens who are convinced that

6

there is nothing narrow about them at all. I find it noteworthy that in the 1980s an historian arms himself not for counterattack by modernists but by fundamentalists. While conservative and militant Protestants have for several years been pointing to a conspiracy to subvert America on the part of humanistic liberals—the current code name for what were once called modernists—there are so few of these around and they are so ill-organized, so dispersed, and so demoralized that one need hardly prepare to take cover when mentioning them pejoratively. The fundamentalists, however, are here in force and are more than ready to engage in polemics against anyone who treads on their territory. My treading I conceive chiefly as analysis. In the spirit of Spinoza, my chief aim is not to laugh or to cry, but to understand. Still, I bid possibly enraged modernists or funda- mentalists to smile their way through this exercise in the fashion of a friend of mine who likes to say, "Well, then, let's agree to disagree. You do things your way and I'll do things God's way."

The second risk has to do with terms. There is danger that unless I take great care in defining, some may confuse modern- ism with modernity, or fundamentalism with evangelicalism or historic Catholic orthodoxy, Protestant-style.

Third, in examining the two alternatives, the dangers of both over- and underestimation of their potency and the crisis they helped produce are very real. To overestimate the crisis would be to play into the hands of partisans who worked hard to create the impression that they embodied all the alternatives available. To underestimate it is to thwart understanding of the way in which these alternatives exercised and can exercise a tyranny over minds and in spirits. This is not the point to argue people out of positions they hold, but to point to the limited numbers of people who hold them—and then to point to the strategic positions they have held in large subcultures in the American past.

Finally, I shall risk being misunderstood by presenting the chronological scheme that locates modernism before fundamen- talism. In the minds of many who express themselves in print, there is an instinct that sees fundamentalism as an instant reac- tion to modernity, a simple perpetuation of historic orthodoxy that then came to be tested by modernists. Viewed close up, however, a different picture develops. At the onset of modernity as it reached the American psyche—however we wish to locate that—some gifted and enterprising people who were highly exposed to world culture immediately set out to adapt, to accommodate themselves to it and to assimilate it to their endeavors. For a half century there were many fence-sitters. Conservative forces were beginning to gather and group around equally gifted and enterprising counterattackers. But it took the better part of a half century for the nascent and inchoate fundamentalist faction to take shape and present itself militantly.

The chronology, then, runs something like this. 1. Modernity occurs, a two-word proposition that will need some unpacking soon. 2. Conservatives instinctively react, but they also appropriate selective elements and make cautious adjustments. 3. Modernists come on the scene, seize initiative, and embrace much of modernity. 4. Fundamentalists, who had met the first challenges in diffuse and sometimes relaxed but always individualized ways, found in modernism a focus for their own organization. 5. By 1925 the two parties were ready to contend in the field monitored by both the ecclesiastical and the public eyes. 6. The legacy of that conflict lives on and finds new life periodically.

When I speak of these options as "limited alternatives," there is an implication that they did not have to be, or that they did not have to be apparently "all there was." The historical case for this can be made by reference to the different patterns responses to modernity took in other places. The German rationalist enlightenment, Hegelian and neo-Kantian follow-ups, and conservative responses were of quite different character from the forces that made up the American pattern. Thus when in 1974 American evangelicals, many of them of fundamentalist tinge and tint, at least in respect to hard-line views of biblical inerrancy, met with European evangelicals at Lausanne, they were surprised to find that fundamentalism was absent from conservative Protestantism on the east side of the Atlantic. Add to this the fact that most American black Protestants are evangelical and biblically based without ever having been fundamentalist, and one can see that people in lineages programmed in different ways had room for different alternatives.

Once modernity struck American life and religion, some sort of response was necessary. The modernists drew on one kind of philosophical lore and the fundamentalists on another. That they may have failed to do full justice to that lore is not to fault them

8

for having tried. The church has often in its history had to deal with apparently alien philosophies. At the risk of great but necessary oversimplification, an oversimplification that builds on a point already made by others and not one that is now being established, we can indicate some examples. A typically Hebraic faith encountered Plato and came up with the classic orthodox Christian creeds against the background of Hellenic and sometimes Platonic thought patterns. In the thirteenth century the enemy of Christianity, the Muslim, brought about a confrontation with and then a critical adoption of the thought of Aristotle, who must have looked like a naturalistic pantheist to Christian theists. Yet, out of it came Catholic orthodox scholastic thought. The church has faced up to, criticized, and appropriated parts of the worlds of Copernicus and Galileo, Freud and Einstein, until these come to be taken for granted by conservatives as well as liberals. All this means in the present case that some sort of response was necessary, but the exact form, including its philosophical elements, was not.

Before launching into the historical case, one more preliminary issue presents itself: what good is all this? Why bother to revisit this crisis? Among many available answers, I would stress four. First, humans have a need to locate themselves, to post landmarks and signposts in a diffuse and confusing culture. Second, such signposting demands discriminations and distinctions. Add to this the fact that designation of landmarks and camps adds to the clarification of one's own location in a culture or among its movements, and that this helps establish and sustain personal identity. Finally, analysis of this sort might help turn inevitable conflict into creative conflict, to make clearer the options of one's own day and thus to be able to help meet a later stage of the ongoing crisis.

Frequently I have already used the word modernity, a word that seems to have as many definitions as it has users. Without for a moment presuming to limit or settle the definitional question, I can at least help us through the present passages by pointing to the ways in which I believe it helped create the circumstances to which modernism and fundamentalism addressed themselves. Those adept at spotting definers of modernity will at once find shadows of giant figures like Max Weber and Talcott Parsons and maybe Emile Durkheim and, closer up, contemporaries like Robert Bellah, Peter Berger, Thomas Luckmann, and John Murray Cuddihy, though none of them need take full responsibility for the way their tradition is here transmitted and, some might say, traduced.

Modernity occurred concurrently with and both as an agent of and a response to a number of "brute facts," processes like industrialization and urbanization. While there were many human continuities, some as old as the Stone Age—for example, religion did not disappear in the face of secularizing forces—something did happen. Today everyone is expected to agree with the jerk of a knee that it is dangerous to overdraw distinctions between traditional and modern cultures, and it is. There was much of modernity in tradition and much tradition in modernity, and one can overdramatize the breaches between the two. Yet, when all the analysis is finished and all bets are hedged, I think it still worthwhile to compare the world in which most of our grandparents lived with the one we inhabit, to perceive some of the changes, be they for better or for worse.

My own grandfather, for instance, was born in the home of a cabinetmaker in Switzerland, in a valley where for centuries his people had the choice of being cabinetmakers or farmers. In the record book in the village church one would find baptisms traceable back to the sixteenth century, all of them in the Reformed tradition, and few villagers would in all their life meet someone of a different faith. Their work and their home were at one place. Their pastor might be aware of remote alternatives, but these neither threatened nor lured them. Something similar would be present in a Catholic city in Spain, a Jewish shtetl in the Pale of Europe, an African tribal constellation, or an Asian setting. Of course, there were cosmopolitan cultures through the ages, but even these usually had a location in a religiously based "host culture" that screened the alternatives.

Modernity, in a phrase of John Murray Cuddihy, sundered primordial ties. Now people chopped apart fact and value, work and home, politics from economy, ethnicity and religion (the Jewish trauma), church and state (the Catholic upheaval), region from faith (the Protestant inconvenience). The technical terms for this "chopping up" process are differentiation, specialization, universalization, and diffusion. And with this chopping up came choice, voluntaryism, the sense of freedom to pick up or drop

10

various options. Peter Berger likes to remind us of a "heretical imperative," recalling that heresy comes from the Greek word for "choice." David Apter has used modern economics to illustrate the process. A couple of centuries ago economics was for people in much of the Western world not so much a matter of fate and inheritance as it was rational calculation. This became a paradigm for the rest of modernity, and brought with it both an exhilarating freedom and a terror of decision. Cuddihy properly, to my taste, points out that this sundering of primordial ties left "wholeness-hunger in its wake."

Modernism and fundamentalism set out to minister to the hunger for wholeness through very different means. Before addressing the modernist version, we should note how this West-wide change came to America by the 1880s. Urbanization entailed not merely the growth of the *civitas*, the civil locale gathered around the holy hill with all roads converging on it, but also *urbs*, the more brutal and bewildering complex of civil and barbarian types gathered for varied purposes. In America this was the new industrial city, which served as a magnet for people of many backgrounds. Second, this urban move was part of what Berger calls a "pluralization of life worlds," the fact that people carried different kinds of mental furnished apartments under their hats, often as a result of the fact that they came from different life worlds in Africa, Asia, and most of all Europe. Add to this the impact of modern media of communication, ever more kinetic and eventually electric, which could bring alien signals into ghetto and shtetl, parish and ward, monastery and academy. The media made possible the conception of a cosmopolitan order, even if people reinforced themselves against many of their signals. And with all these other turns, there came theological choice, freedom to choose faith commitments, thanks to republican or democratic innovations that had to do with separated church and state, distinguished religious and civil spheres. Revivalists, in this picture, were not merely bearers of "the old time religion," but impellers of modernity because they did not assume an intact covenant but bade people to choose, to decide to help constitute one.

One needs religious rationales for changes as drastic as these, and old religions tailored themselves or left a void which new or quasi-religions filled. Some of these were ideologies like progres-

11

sivism and Marxism, forces that in Cuddihy's vision were "dedifferentiating," or demodernizing, because they by some measure of coercion tried to bring again the sense of wholeness to society, culture, and person. (Curiously, if we wish to be free to play with words, 'modernism' is in this sense demodernizing!) Without some religious rationale people are likely to be swept away by change, become desolate and shipwrecked, and vulnerable to being overwhelmed.

In the course of the nineteenth century in America we can see two sets of options for this ministry to the hunger for wholeness. One was innovative, eager to break up existing forms of family and economic life and to start anew, usually in organic and integral communities that gathered people with a universal vision into a parochial center. One thinks of the communities of utopians, Shakers, Oneidans, or Mormons in this group. Joseph Smith, the Mormon founder, announced that he had been told to reject all the existing options and restore or help restore in the latter-days the long-hidden church of Jesus Christ. Some through Christian Science addressed the issue with a kind of gnosis that provided an encompassing outlook on reality that helped adherents cope with change. Spiritualism, theosophy, New Thought, all addressed wholeness-hunger with idea patterns that departed from most ties to tradition.

For most citizens, however, there was no need to reach to arcane and esoteric locales for an address to their needs. The symbolic pools available to them were able to be drawn upon and transformed. British social philosopher Ernest Gellner has shown to at least my satisfaction that "all things being equal," which means short of total revolution, complex societies find it convenient and even necessary to make their moves by reworking symbols that they carried with them "over the hump of transition" to the society they inhabit and the social contract they have approved. Marx may not recognize Marxism in societies that insist on making their changes in the light of Marxian revolution—one thinks of how much Lenin, Stalin, and Mao traduced Marx. Similarly, Jewish-Christian, postbiblical societies make their moves in light of at least blurry recall of symbols associated with their heritage. In America the approved social contract came in a combination of biblical and Enlightenment thought, whose symbols seem capable of almost infinitely varied reformulation.

So it was that people who were possessed by traditions that they did not fully possess began to reexamine their symbols. The conservatives became very busy just as conservatives always must when there is change: this is G. K. Chesterton's familiar picture of the industry it takes to keep a white fence post white. One does not merely let it alone, but one strenuously counterattacks against environmental change to the post. If the fundamentalists chose that exercise, the modernists chose to cut new posts out of the same wood, but to locate them differently. In their view the conservative approach was time-buying but finally futile. They wanted to seize initiative in the name of faith.

Forget the fence post and think of another image. The conservatives, as they became fundamentalists, wove a kind of cocoon around their subcultures. A cocoon is "a covering of fibrous material spun by the larvae . . . as protection. . . ." The result is an enclosure that is translucent, not dark, but still protective, cozy, warm, and capable of creating an illusion that all the life there is is within it. Robert Wiebe has spoken of America as a "segmented society" in which people could live together by living apart. This response to modernity made it possible for those inside the webbing to ignore, explain away, or distance themselves from "the others." Theologically, this usually meant that others were not of the elect or were drop-outs from the approved millennial scheme. Ghetto Catholicism, in the eyes of recent refugees from it, was both a warmly nurturing and a confining "cocoon," which had Jewish and Protestant counterparts. There one takes life "whole" but does so by what some sociologists call "pluralistic ignorance" and I would call "ignoring of pluralism" in its deepest assaults.

The other choice, which some might see as simply the weaving of a larger, more flexible, less fibrous, and more nearly transparent cocoon, was the modernist. For all its failures to do so, this culture intended to be cosmopolitan in outlook, unafraid of pluralism. It sought to provide shelter and wholeness by a cosmic, inclusive ideological outlook which was capable of getting perspective in the face of all assaults and absorbing all blows. If I were to trade once more on an image of John Murray Cuddihy, these cosmopolites were much like people who ride an airplane

13

above the hurricane and look down on it with full awareness of its force but still safe from its strongest push by the fact that interpretation gave them perspective and distance. It is time to put these riders-above-the-hurricane in our sights and focus more clearly on them as "modernists."

Modernism appeared in Judaism as well as in Christianity, in Catholicism as well as in Protestantism. Enlightenment Judaism from Europe took shape in Reform, the predominant organized or organizing party of chiefly German Jews at the beginning of our period. The orthodox who came later, when they became aware of Reform at all, considered it to be something like Protestant Unitarianism, a betrayal of Jewish peoplehood and tradition. Roman Catholic modernism in Europe addressed some of the issues of the kind of modernism we encounter in America. But despite efforts by some Vaticanists to condemn it with the tag "Americanism," little modernism reached America and even less was homegrown here. A Notre Dame professor or two, the members of a religious order or two who produced a journal or three—all these were very important for the later history of Roman Catholicism, but they were not ominous or promising cultural presences over against which it was profitable for American Catholic intransigents to organize. The modernism of our story was chiefly a late nineteenth- and early twentieth-century Anglo-American development that included at least these eight elements:

First, it was an attempt to satisfy the hunger for wholeness after the modern sunderings had occurred. Old-world views were breaking up, old moorings and landmarks lost, and some articulators sensed a need for an inclusive, encompassing outlook that would have intellectual as well as spiritual satisfactions.

The theology of such a movement had to aspire to the cosmic in an age of cosmic daring. If Darwin was describing an older world and the new cosmologists a larger universe than hitherto pictured, the old images of God needed expansion. If culture contacts brought an awareness of rich anthropological variety, then one had to take Jesus "out of the box" that the culture had used to locate him and through some spiritual redefinition find a Jesus-like or Christic outlook for all cultures.

This outlook, partly by accident and partly by intention, was imperial. While spelled out chiefly by people we today call WASPs at the height of their hubris, when it seemed that all the world could be civilized on one model, these definers and prescribers set out to present a theology and style that could be normative.

Fourth, modernism was progressivist, optimistic, trading on a not always acknowledged metaphysics of progress when the empirical situation seemed to go against it. Lyman Abbott, journalist among the modernists, could say of World War I that now and then in its inevitable upward climb the human race might stumble. Then it needed a bandage on the knee and could resume the climb. Needless to say, Walter Rauschenbusch and others tempered this optimism with more realistic visions, yet the modernists used Kingdom of God language to describe a motion, a thrust in history that could not be denied.

Modernism was intentionally therapeutic and pastoral, even in the hands of intellectuals. Most of them worked out their own mild crisis in its terms, and extrapolated on the basis of this hoping that it might reach the "common people." The princes of the pulpit in the age, men like Henry Ward Beecher, gained significant and even enormous popular followings as they presented a cushioner for the shock of modernity.

Sixth, modernism was passionately scientific, for it embraced what it took to be the key mark of the age, a love of science. Men like William Rainey Harper, founding president of the University of Chicago, never tired of propagating the idea that Christians had nothing to fear and much to gain from scientific progress. The modernists saw their theology to be empirical, its methods satisfying the criteria of modern scientific inquiry.

Penultimately, the modernists were critical. They were not afraid of what was ahead. They did not need or at least did not realize the need for a cocoon. They wanted to be in universities, communication centers, at junctures of commerce and industry, wherever change was occurring. They did not want to absorb all change without criticism, but they also did not want their own method and outlook to lack critical sensitivity.

And modernism was developmental. I shy away here for the moment from the temptation to make "evolution" the key word, since latterly evolution is equated with Charles Darwin. Most modernists were not Darwinian so much as they were neo-

15

Lamarckian, since "natural selection" seemed too random for their purposive metaphysic. But they did not even need to make neo-Lamarckianism the center of their philosophical outlook, and some of them had more vague quasi-Hegelian developmental views in mind. They *did* move decisively from static concepts of the universe toward dynamic, from changeless or entropic (à la Henry Adams) to teleological and purposive. One might almost apply to them the dream of Teilhard de Chardin and a title of Flannery O'Connor: "everything that rises must converge," and all was rising.

From a distance, and most Americans kept a distance, the would-be cosmopolitan modernists were themselves spinners of another cocoon. Outsiders knew precisely where to locate them. Most of them were exemplars of New England theology transformed, heirs of Horace Bushnell and other fashionable anti-revivalist church leaders. They were churchly, ready to contend for the future of denominations that today we call mainline. They spun their cocoons in theological schools at the brand new universities, and occupied virtually every intellectual center that favored or made room for religion. At home with Max Weber's *Rationalität*, they became managers and bureaucrats and were the natural leaders of complex denominational and proto-ecumenical agencies. They were at home cross-culturally and naturally gravitated toward missionary leadership roles even though they lost passion for jungle and beachhead themselves. Similarly, they were editors, publishers, diarists, travellers, people equipped and eventually privileged to be in the eye of the hurricane and not in the huts in its path.

Much of modernism was clerical; it is uncertain how widespread was lay support. David Lewis, a recent dissertation writer at the University of Chicago, traced a generation of inchoate modernists-fundamentalists in turn-of-the-century Chicago, a city in which the battles were to become intense and the lines harshly drawn. He found the laity faced with a confusion of directives and thus bound for anomie, people who were seizing the moment to enjoy being converted or ministered to by old-time evangelists like Dwight L. Moody while their minds and sensibilities were attracted to modernizers like William Rainey Harper, a few miles south of Moodydom at the university campus. After a generation most of them felt a need to take sides, though I suspect

16

that an evangelical heart beats in the bodies of most mainline Christians, while many evangelicals short of strident fundamentalism find intellectual satisfactions in some of the adjustments that look modernist.

The modernist subculture that wanted to be inclusive was more at home with secular culture than were the antecedents of fundamentalism. Those who sought exposure found some and were visible to editors of *Scribner's* and *Harper's, North American Review* and *Atlantic.* The progenitors of fundamentalism seemed to be behind the times in antiscientific backwoods and antimodern backwaters. This is not to say that the modernist outlook went uncriticized; many an editor found a following for pointing to embarrassments in the modernist compromise or for claiming that the adapters were selling out the historic faith.

By the way, to my knowledge all the modernists were brought up evangelically. Modernism was not a converting impulse, despite its belief that right-thinking people would see its light. Interestingly, most of the leaders more or less eased into modernism. Some of them had or expressed a kind of fashionable Victorian doubt during their mid-passage from the conservative cocoon toward cosmopolitanism. Exuberance, however, more than inner torment marks the diaries and memoirs of the era.

Modernism was an outlook on life and theology, and we should point to a few characteristic marks of that theology. The historians of the movement, William Hutchison, Bernard Meland, Lloyd Averill, Kenneth Cauthen—their ranks are still few—have pointed to subtleties that my broad brush does not allow for, and they might even take exception to some accents. But wide reading in the sources and in their resources leads me to accent several.

While it might seem strange to stress that a theology was theistic, such stress is necessary here. Whatever else they came up with, theirs was a theism, with deism only revived at the outer Ethical Culture or Free Religious edges of the otherwise Protestant Christian movement. That is, for some modernists like philosopher John Fiske, God was becoming a name for an impersonal force, not someone to be addressed. But when most modernists prayed, they focused on a Thou who was responsive, even if this Thou was assigned far more tasks than the somewhat domesticable pre-modern deity was responsible for. The theistic stress is remarkable further because it ran counter to so many Enlightenment-era forecasts. A century earlier "when wise men hoped," they hoped for an era in which rationality would win out. No longer would people need what a new age called a projection of their wishes or desires, a Father in the heavens above.

The modernists, perhaps perpetuating their Sunday school "genetic programming," seldom wavered in their belief in a somehow personal and ever more expansive God. Whether as providence, progress, or process, this God was addressable as well as expressible. To the wavering soul or threatened intellect, the modernists could speak reassuringly. While the Abbott-Beecher code phrase, "Evolution is God's way of doing things," says both too little and too much, it says something about the way the modernists could roll with every punch. Biblical criticism was not a problem but an opportunity, since it situated ancient Scriptures in the human and social environments which enhanced the revelatory and redemptive venture. This theism, let it be noted, was immanental. The transcendent deity was not so much "wholly other" as at home in cosmic and earthly processes. The modernists did what they could to minimize the line between nature and supernature, finite and infinite.

Second, modernism was surprisingly Christic. It may well be that this was the least thought out, least well-developed aspect of their thought. Now it happens that a cosmic Christology is easily available in Johannine and Pauline writings and belongs to the language of piety, liturgy, and theology through the ages. But that it appears in modernism does not seem simply accountable for, except again in the programming the modernist articulators received in childhood nurture. It is not surprising to see that an evolutionary theistic philosopher turns suddenly kerygmatic, proclamatory, from another compartment of the mind, erupting in proper names that interrupt and give a climax to process. But the modernists did not think they were turning or being interruptive at all. Jesus of Nazareth, a rabbinic figure in history at the eastern end of the Mediterranean among a not-much-account people at no particular moment in history, should have been able to be swallowed up in later stages of Hegelian dialectic or Lamarckian adaptation. Yet, for all their belief in progress, Jesus was to them somehow normative, still unfolding, still ahead, but also the center or focus. Today theologies from Teilhard's to

18

latter-day Whiteheadianisms have ways of "making this come out right," but one gets little impression that modernists struggled much with the problem. They encountered new religions, or at least once-distant religions, like Hinduism, and immediately found the Christ-principle or the ethics of Jesus operative there, without telling others exactly how or why. This expansive view, by the way, led to a diminishing of the evangelistic or missionary outlook in the course of a generation. The modernists would graft traditions, not superimpose or displace, yet somehow there was confidence that Christ-ianity or Jesus-ology would survive and win out.

In this trinitarian scheme, the modernists were also spiritual. Their socio-political counterparts in the concurrent Social Gospel movement did not seem to be at home with socialism because of its materialism, and these New Theologians were not fully at home with the more straight-out secular philosophies of the day because the philosophers detected the Christian spirituality that eluded others. Not many modernist theologians wrote prayers as eloquent as those of Social Gospel thinker Walter Rauschenbusch, but they preached and prayed and some of them, like Washington Gladden, at the juncture of the movements, or Harry Emerson Fosdick in the later stages of modernism, did write hymns that are still sung. But their spirituality had a kind of wan aspect of the sort we associate with the liberal temper. There was little of the Dostoevskian tumult or saintly and mystical striving in this genteel spirituality.

In this trinitarian scheme one might also add holiness to spirituality as a final point. Modernism was passionate at least about morality and ethics, fitting as it did into a kind of neo-Kantian mold. Let modernity take away some aspects of faith, the modernists would serve society and universe by impelling goodness. The Fatherhood of God and the Brotherhood of Man, fused with the coming of the kingdom, evoked moral response. There was little antinomianism or libertinism in this form of modernism.

The modernists made use of the tools of their age and did not fear, indeed they delighted in, the two that led fundamentalists to their most focused reaction. They appropriated a version of evolutionary-developmentalism and they believed that only the historical and critical approach to the Bible could rescue it for a new age. The critical approach was a matter of integrity and truth. But it was also useful, since it led to an enlargement of vision, and would attract the undecided, the irreligious who were put off by biblical contradiction and unnatural miracle. While the acceptance of the term "critical" may have been the biggest theological public relations blunder in American Protestant history, the modernists were sincere in their belief that criticism was building, not destroying, in intent and effect.

Modernism had its era, and came to a kind of social triumph just before World War I and a theological climax in the mid-twenties. The shattering effect of World War I on European theology, an effect that helped occasion theologies of crisis and criticisms of a culture of humanism, was slower to reach America. Not until the early 1930s, during the depression, did "neoorthodoxy" and thus antimodernism gain a wide hearing, chiefly in the same elites, the same sectors of the theological economy. Then came the time for pointing to failures in the well-intentioned modernist program.

The modernist-fundamentalist controversy came to a head in denominational battles among northern Baptists, Presbyterians, Disciples of Christ, and others in the mid-twenties and received its stereotyping caricature in the Scopes trial in Tennessee in 1925. The fundamentalists were so far beyond the pale of modernist discourse that they had no effect at all in causing modernists to waver or their cause to crumble. The crumbling came from within the camp, or from humanists around it.

Suddenly, it was clear that the progressive world view was not doing justice to the perdurable dimensions of the demonic in existence. The Christological thinking had been facile and did not stand up against neoorthodoxy's probes and proclamations. The anthropology was judged superficial by the Niebuhrians of a new age who with theological finesse, but pedagogical naiveté, restored the language of Original Sin. The failure to evangelize led to a dwindling of the movement and was part of what historian Robert Handy has called a "religious depression" during the economic depression. Politically, modernists were to lose out when the lay masses clung to the uncriticized Bible, to which every fundamentalist or conservative could appeal for scoring points. And modernist piety did not do justice, for all its pantheistic logic, to the deepest yearnings of many hearts.

Was its collapse a cultural crisis? It was certainly part of the

20

crisis in that, by posing itself against fundamentalism, it helped exhaust alternatives when the people in the culture needed more. The collapse of a progressivist outlook led to floundering. The decline of the WASP elite in the midst of pluralism left a void that only less genteel forces were equipped to fill. Modernism produced not a single genius, no Jonathan Edwards or John Courtney Murray, no William James or Reinhold Niebuhr, no giant who people feel called upon to read for the power of his or her mind as they do other articulators of thought patterns not in vogue, and this fact has made even the heritage of modernism difficult to grasp.

Modernism then was supplanted by liberalism, which picked up the more moderate side of nineteenth-century evangelicalism, or neoorthodoxies which impelled their holders to keep up cultural contact but to do so more critically. The still-attacking fundamentalists are not wholly wrong in one aspect of their vision. Those who walk from a precritical into a critical mental furnished apartment "cannot go home again." They are rarely, if ever, "born again" to the world of their original naiveté, and when they convert they feel a need to constrict, to shore up defenses, to build boundaries around the mind and stop asking the questions. When there is a rare conversion in that direction, the colleagues of the convert spend less time speaking of a miracle of the spirit or a theological turn than of the need for a psychiatrist or a social analyst. The modernist impulse turns critical or self-critical; it does not produce returnees to fundamentalism among converts from it, at least not on a wide scale.

The legacy of modernism is necessarily mixed. Critics today accuse it of overadapting, of striving too much to be relevant to external norms at the neglect of the inner impulses of faith and theology. They congratulate it for not accepting modernity passively, for taking initiative and pointing to choice. Even the critic must note the ingenuity and persistence with which modernists reached into the Christian repository of options rather than go elsewhere. If the modernists are to be criticized for their hubris, they held to this deadly sin less rewardingly than did their fundamentalist counterparts. They were pastoral and therapeutic about the head's and the heart's reasons. Their political naiveté was astonishing: they thought they were winning and would and could win. They failed to pick up significant secular allies, since most humanists came to see them as barterers away of the faith they equated conveniently with unattractive fundamentalism.

The attraction of modernism is largely over. In the secular theology of Protestantism, the sort associated with people like Harvey Cox in the mid-1960s, there was a critical rebirth, just as I have implied there are continuities with Teilhard de Chardin, who appealed to far more than Catholics. One cannot say that modernism in chastened form will not reappear, but in the early 1980s the cultural predispositions around the churches are not conductive, and the inner impulses of theologians toward it are not strong.

THE FUNDAMENTALIST ATTRACTION, 1925-1980

Fundamentalism is the code name or party label for the equally complex counterpart to modernism in the cultural crisis that I have labelled a "tyranny of limited alternatives." To deed it the second half of the century of American modernity would seem or could be historically naive, psychologically perverse, politically capitulative, and strategically unwise. By that I mean to say that the public relations of current exemplars of fundamentalism who claim their tens of millions and aspire to hundreds of millions have to be taken with many qualifications and all ten fingers crossed. For all their ecclesiastical power in conservative Protestantism and their growing political weight, they remain a part of one subculture in a still very diverse and pluralistic society. As a formal, organized force fundamentalism meets very definite limits under a low ceiling or inside a confining corral. In Lincolnian terms, "for those who like that sort of things, that is the sort of thing they do like."

While the Gallup Poll can find scores of millions of people who, when asked, find that it now occurs to them that, yes, they were "born again," this does not mean that they should all be located in the fundamentalist camp. Pentecostalists, evangelicals, and confessionalists may find some sympathy for and common cause with fundamentalist attacks on leftover modernism. But they do not need it for the articulation of their own vision, and for all their cognitive agreements on some basic Protestant teachings, they do not hold them the same way. Nor do they reinforce them with stand-offish attitudes and behavior patterns characteristic of those that fundamentalism cherishes, nurtures, and propagates.

Beyond that conservative Protestant core, few in "mainline" Protestantism are attracted to much if anything in the fundamentalist package. Traditionalist Catholics often express admiration from a distance for the fact that, by God, fundamentalists at least really believe something while liberals are wishy-washy, and

23

while their social programs sometimes match, up close they find no reason to let fundamentalists instruct them or speak for them. Jews in defense of Israel often welcome the pro-Israel premillennialism of most fundamentalists and now and then hand out awards as a way of saying thanks, but there is little intellectual communion or behavioral overlap at the awards banquets. Even orthodox Jews are far from fundamentalism in practice. Needless to say, the secular half of most Americans or the secular half of America finds nothing attractive in fundamentalism except, now and then, when violent-minded humanists speak up in admiration for religionists who care enough to be militants, to have crusades. Such a taunting humanism likes to distance itself from religious claims by seeing fundamentalism, because of its very implausibility, as the normative and encompassing "historic Christianity." Yet that form of humanism is sophisticated and rare in the culture. Fundamentalism is not a temptation for the majority.

Having said all that, it is also true that fundamentalism as a movement does cut a wide swath in conservative Protestantism and is a cultural and now a political presence. In a moment we shall assess ways in which it fits into surging movements around the world. And the presence of those movements helps lend credibility to my otherwise crazy chronology in which modernism is the first reaction to modernity and fundamentalism the more powerful second wave. To put as bold a stamp as possible on it: I know of nowhere in the world today where empathy, tolerance, responsiveness, and other liberal-modernist virtues (if one dare call them virtues now) are prevailing over against dedifferentiating, demodernizing ideologies or social movements. If one wants to buy stock, he or she would be well advised to pursue cocoon builders more than cosmopolites. The ministry to the hunger for wholeness occurs less at the moment through appeals to cosmic theology than to cozy and tribalist enclosures where that which is disruptive is kept from view and used negatively when used at all.

From Baylor to Berkeley, from Boulder to Boston, in any urban university setting, one can feel free to attack modernism with impunity. To call fundamentalism into question demands a mite of courage and a willingness to answer some angry mail. Resistance to development and evolution has become an issue in a thousand school districts. Rejection of biblical criticism is one of the more potent means of gathering support for control of even moderate denominations.

All of these trends, if I am reading them correctly in and around fundamentalism and church cultures, run counter to most predictions and projections of the past two centuries. Monsieur Guyau could write of the nonreligion of the future. David Hume and Immanuel Kant and their successors could undercut the noumenal basis of conservative faiths. Benjamin Franklin and Thomas Jefferson helped establish a universalizing reasonable religion of the republic that would prevail when all grew wise. The bearded giants of the nineteenth century may not have shared "the heavenly city of the eighteenth century" enlightened dreamers, but these stormy god-killers did not picture supernatural revelation surviving as people formed new social movements.

Religion was to decline; yet it has prospered, and is a major motive power behind most of the wars—ethnic-racial-cultural-national though they also be—that plague our day. One style of *ratio* was to have prevailed with the scientific and enlightened outlook, yet a jet aircraft with 340 passengers is probably conveying 340 world views to a destination. Even scientists are not sure of "the scientific world view." Humanism is in disarray, and the children of the cultured only a decade and more ago formed an antihumanist, antirationalist, antiscientific counterculture of studied barbarianism. And if people expected that modernism would lead to the protean style of psyche which can adapt to and absorb everything, it underestimated the alternative constrictive personality that screened out all signals but one. Finally, while many looked for an ecumenical convergence ("global village," "spaceship earth," "new creation as metropolis," WCC and UN and UWF), everywhere there seems to be what Harold Isaacs has called a massive and convulsive ingathering of peoples into their separatenesses and over-againstnesses, usually with religious reinforcement of tribe.

After the defeat of Senator Goldwater in 1964, the foremost secular historian of the revivalist impulse in America, William G. McLoughlin, spoke for most analysts when he pictured the subsequent demise of political fundamentalism. During the next few years of militancy and counterculture it seemed to have no possible future. But since then the Nixon, Ford, Carter, and beginning

Reagan presidencies have been anything but modernist in outlook and, while never fundamentalist in religion or politics, knew that fundamentalism was a force to be reckoned with, fended off, or exploited. Whatever the dimensions of the New Christian Right—and they are bigger than many foresaw and smaller than its leaders claim—it is certainly the strongest intrusion into politics by the fundamentalists since at least the Christian Anti-Communist Crusades of earlier cold-war times and in the McCarthy period. In sum, our topic is not irrelevant; even if it were, there is intrinsic value in assessing the American mind-set of 1925 as a contribution to understanding past cultural crises.

Without wanting to stain American fundamentalism with a brush tarred in unlovely international movements, it is not unfair to say that the fundamentalist ethos does have counterparts elsewhere and that there are some things to learn about present-day America by looking elsewhere. Most controversially, but not without the promise of some understanding, Americans have seen in Shi'ite Islamic movements in Iran a dedifferentiating and demodernizing impulse that has some parallels in American fundamentalism. It weaves a cocoon around its people; and Sūnni Muslims, Baha'i heretics, or ethnic Kurds, to say nothing of Jews and Christians and Americans, have little or no status in its theocratic vision and clerisy. The people in the huts have struck back at the riders above the eye of the hurricane. The intellectual and fiscal elites who became world citizens and got most of the mixed benefits of modernity were unseated by Iranians who reclad themselves in the *chador* and ruled out intrusive cosmopolitan signals.

There is a fundamentalist outlook in *soka gakkai* in Japan, in the Islamic-Hindu conflict of Kerala and West Bengal, and in the religious dimensions of ethnic strife in Catholic-Protestant Northern Ireland. The *Gush Emunim* in Israel use the Bible exactly as American fundamentalists do to state their territorial West Bank claims, and Muslim fundamentalists reply in kind. American fundamentalism may be unarmed and may include many people who lack such belligerency, and American pluralism is too rich to permit lining up across trenches or in various sectors of city or nation. So it would be absurd and reprehensible to prophesy the coming of an American fascism on fundamentalist soil. The comparison here is strictly to the tribal impulse, the ethno- or religio-centrism of the elect, and most of all to dedifferentiation or demodernization as an attempt to retain or restore some sort of personal and social "wholeness" in the face of assaults.

That these tribal and ethnic movements have such a religious cast has surprised many, not least of all in America. But here as elsewhere a sort of resacralization has gone on. British sociologist Bryan Wilson would deny this because the nation does not live by a single set of sacral symbols. But the American Daniel Bell, aware of the hugeness of subcultures, has argued more plausibly that subcultures can resacralize. He has pointed to the high-intensity mythic and mystic subculture among the children of elites. From them are recruited the "new religions" and their adherents, the cults, the occultists. Much larger is the "redemptive" or "traditional" mainline culture which has become more conscious, if in a benign and undefensive spirit, of its own need for "roots," for whatever gives its people a social identity. But most surprisingly potent is what Bell designates as the "evangelical" and "moralistic" subculture of which fundamentalism is a part.

Did fundamentalism present a cultural crisis in 1925 when its consolidation became visible and when it was apparently defeated in denominational contest and symbolically in the Scopes trial? Does it represent a cultural crisis at the end of the period, 1980? I argue that it does because it has effectively diminished the sense of alternatives for millions of Americans, and has attracted enough millions of people who in one corner of their hearts or minds reject ecumenical Christianity, interreligious empathy, and republican pluralism. Ten years ago Dean Kelley wrote a book on why conservative churches are growing, a chronicle of why mainline ones were failing. His fastest-growers were mostly "fundamentalist" in mind-cast, though not in doctrinal orthodoxy. Black Muslims, Orthodox Jews, Seventh-Day Adventists, Jehovah's Witnesses, Church of Christ, Latter-day Saints and their kind might include notable citizens, but together they could not constitute the republic off which they live and in which they thrive, to say nothing of an ecumenical movement they would abhor.

One way to minimize the dimensions of the fundamentalist-induced crisis is to be careful about definitions and not to lump

27

people together. I have already begun to do this by ruling out secular, humanistic, Jewish, Catholic, and mainline Protestant peoples, but there is still more need for discrimination in the conservative Protestant camp.

First of all, not all evangelicals are fundamentalists (and not all evangelicals want to be evangelicals; witness the Southern Baptist Convention's regular appeals to be regarded autochthonously and not as a species of the genus evangelical). Were one to line up a check list of doctrines that putatively constitute fundamentalism's fundamentals, including the Virgin Birth of Jesus, the substitutionary blood atonement, the physical resurrection, the second coming, and the like, it is hard to picture many people wanting to call themselves evangelical without their being eager to affirm these teachings alongside fundamentalism. There might be some parting over the particular philosophical grounding of fundamentalism's insistent passion for "inerrancy" of the Bible. Many evangelicals speak of "limited inerrancy," criticize the philosophical a priorism that led to inerrancy in the nineteenth century, or insist that they have higher views of biblical authority than those crimped and cramped by inerrantism. And not all evangelicals share the kinds of premillennialism which mark much of fundamentalism. If we recognize that our deepest behavioral patterns are grounded in our deepest beliefs, it is safest to go on and say that the more marked and more profound separations between larger evangelicalism and fundamentalism are behavioral and attitudinal. Billy Graham is being evangelical when he welcomes the Roman Catholic and mainline Methodist bishops to sponsorship and stage presence at his rallies. Fundamentalists are being fundamentalist when they scorn him for having nothing to gain and everything to lose by co-appearance with such betrayers or humanists. Evangelicals ordinarliy have more positive views of the surrounding culture and characteristically support liberal arts colleges while fundamentalists—the line is not neat, but it is there—favor colleges that are more properly Bible institutes, where the humanities are suspect or have no intrinsic value.

Within fundamentalism, of course, there are also many styles. Not all are obsessed with dispensationalism or premillennialism. Millions shrug off or reject the political militancy of much current leadership and remain independent, apolitical, or holders of coincident positions without acknowledging instructions from the New Christian Right. Many mind their own business without being noisy or organized about it. They think you "just might have a point" when you disagree with them and are both committed *and* civil in a day when the heirs of modernism look civil without commitment and activist fundamentalists are committed but not civil.

If some detected a condescending tone about modernism—I hope it was not there, since the historian should seek to understand people in the context of the possibilities of their day and not serve as hanging judge all the time—they might also have spotted a wariness, an impulse to circumscribe and to quarantine in my dealing with fundamentalists. Here I should make clear that this historical and critical analysis is not designed to stigmatize the people called fundamentalists; "some of my friends," if not my best friends, are fundamentalists. More important, there is no intention here to be destructive of faith. While I do not share the fundamentalist outlook, it will soon become clear that I do not find it more implausible than many more respectable ones with which it has been contemporary, and have been rather vigorous about supporting its claims for respectable consideration in the academy.

The chief motive—beyond the Spinozan one cited above, the goal of understanding—that lies behind my desire not to be destructive has to do with my own perception of the hard-wonness, the fragility and gossamer character of life in a cocoon or, better, in a world view held by one's self and significant others. It puzzles me to see American academics treating the rest of the world as an anthropological zoo of endangered species which missionaries should never reach and scholars should always affirm, and then turning against millions of Americans as if they were basilisks under the planks, or agents of botulism in the American fare. It may be true that the attempt to set fundamentalism in perspective might be viewed as destructive by those who oppose perspectival approaches and see themselves uniquely exempt from contingency in history. On the other hand, I have to take the risk that it will be only reinforcing of life inside the cocoon, which will then only be spun thicker to keep me and my kind at a distance. The scholar cannot simply calculate odds, but can try to be fair to evidences and clear about argument.

29

To be told that one has a world view and then to come to agree is to *have* a new world view, and that can be an assault on the fundamentalist heirs of Scottish Common Sense Realism who believe that they can have a rational grasp of the reality that is, *as* it is, without intervening "structure of mind." So, if there is an assault in analysis, let me ingratiate myself to any fundamentalist readers by pointing to some compensating intentions. I believe this is a good moment to study fundamentalism. The structuralist, synchronic, and "binary" approaches to the study of religion have made the world views of Cargo Cultists in Melanesia plausible and respectable. Why can they not be used to show something of the structure and function or hold of premillennial futures? The sociological discernment of a "pluralization of life worlds" has provided instruments for gaining empathy for the occult and esoteric faiths; could it be that it might also lead to new understandings of the more widely held fundamentalisms? The assault by some schools of thought on what I call "nothing buttery," psychological reductionism, might help us buy time against those who have the impulse to see fundamentalism as "nothing but" an attempt to project a potent father as God. And trends in ethnic history that have legitimated curiosity about Carpatho-Rusyns and Hidatsas might one day reach to the point that we historians can make contemporaries positively curious, curious in positive ways, about millions of Americans in an ethnic stock called WASP fundamentalist.

Historians are just these years beginning the task of tracking fundamentalists from their defeats and disgraces in 1925 to their new prosperity in the past decade. Not all fundamentalists would say, of course, that the performance of William Jennings Bryan at Dayton, Tennessee, in 1925 was a disgrace just because nonfundamentalists considered it so. The opprobrium of the outsider can be a reinforcer of the respectability of the group. But the more patient observers then and scholars now, including the author of this essay—a kind of Nebraska-populist-in-boyhood now half grown up—have had to see the Bryan of 1925 as a senile hulk of the man he had been, the kind of fanatic who redoubled his effort as he lost sight of his aim, the old campaigner on a pathetic last campaign. Yet, even as hulk there was some charm in his entanglements with Clarence Darrow. And for some of us, the gasp of recognition of Bryan's leftover integrity when he made some concessions that the most ardent fundamentalist precisionists had to deny. In the eyes of most churches and all the world beyond fundamentalism, in any case, Bryan lost and fundamentalism suffered cultural disdain. The new image was that of lickspittle, mud-booted obscurantists—far from the refinements of fundamentalist scholars like ex-Princetonian J. Gresham Machen.

Similarly, the efforts to take over denominations led to qualified defeats and many, including disgruntled Presbyterians, moved off into the fissiparous actions that produced ever smaller, newer, purer fundamentalist Presbyterianism. Where they lost the seminaries, the fundamentalists built no-account Bible schools and lost academic respectability. For almost two decades one could dismiss them.

They did not dismiss themselves, and it is with this fact that historians now busy themselves. The Bible schools began to be colleges and seminaries and to gain academic responsibility. Some of them fused refined fundamentalism with inherited evangelicalism of a sort that had never joined the fundamentalist party. A generation later the Association of Theological Schools found Fuller, Trinity, Gordon-Conwell, and Asbury, to say nothing of Southern Baptist seminaries that were never securely in fundamentalist camps, to be thriving and aspiring toward ever more expansive visions. While mainline Protestants were content to take the gleanings of "public service time" on the new instrument of radio, conservative Catholics and Lutherans like Father Coughlin and Reverend Walter A. Maier built clienteles and made room for their even less churchly celebrity counterparts to scramble for support and master the medium in their subcultures. The next time anyone looked, their heirs in the electronic church were raising as many millions *each* as all but the top three denominational headquarters were each raising in America. While the fundamentalist revivalists took to the dust and sawdust with the likes of racists like Mordecai Ham, the Hams converted people like Billy Graham who came to be ever more civil, ecumenical, and evangelical—until long-dismissed revivalism came to be at home in pluralist America and Graham golfed with presidents and became in every Gallup poll the most admired (nonpresidential) American year after year. And if the evangelists could not win denominations or inform the mainline

31

ecumenical movement, they could regather as they did in 1942 in a National Association of Evangelicals and set out with new confidence to win, if not America, then Americans.

Every movement I have described, the respectable seminaries, evangelization programs, and ecumenical forces—with a possible and ambiguous exception being the whole of the electronic church—meant a compromising of fundamentalism. Each move had a dimension of access to the main line about it. When Gerald Ford, Jimmy Carter, and Ronald Reagan identify themselves as evangelicals, evangelicalism is not marginal to the culture—the White House remains a bully if now bullied pulpit. And each movement therefore also left hard-core fundamentalism partly behind as a negative reference point. This served to give it a hunger to improve its techniques and organize its adherents' passions to compensate, to grow, as it often has. So here are both evangelicalism and fundamentalism, kissing cousins cognitively and feuding brothers and sisters behaviorally, thriving in the 1980s.

The fundamentalist appeal is to deny the *Zeitgeist*, but toward the end of the half century under scrutiny here it played into the *Zeitgeist*. The public wanted roots, and fundamentalism convinced many that it had unbroken ties to roots in the Bible. People wanted respect and recognition, and fundamentalism convinced them that humanists, elitists, and intellectuals who had despised them were despised of God while God honored the "not many wise" in the culture. They wanted to rise in social class, and fundamentalism motivated them toward material success and promise. They wanted new experiences and, while ordinarily denying tongue-speaking and other charismatic signs, fundamentalism pushed "born-again" impulses toward almost mystical levels of intensity. And most of all—for all the tightrope-walking to which modernity called them—they wanted the net of authority and the inerrant Bible to be wielded as weapons, as much as assurances, against all "compromising" comers.

Perhaps the concern for showing continuities in fundamentalism and pointing to its survival pulls us away from the opposite issue: to account for the late date for the consolidation of fundamentalism around 1925. This runs counter to the usual picture in which Charles Darwin published *The Origin of the Species* in 1859, and by 1860, with knee jerks, all conservative Protestants in America had turned fundamentalistically reactive. Or that Strauss's *Life of Jesus* was translated in 1846, and by 1847 there was massive awareness and resistance. Such accounts give no play to cultural lag, transatlantic delay, apathy, preoccupation, creative foot-dragging, difficulty in putting a name on a threat, or confusion about learning who is in one's party.

Most research into the roots of fundamentalism today is showing that for a half century, while neo-Lamarckians prevailed in the scientific academy until the end of the century, not all conservative Protestants were utterly anti-evolutionist. Dwight L. Moody did not kick theistic evolutionist Henry Drummond off stage any more than he parted company with biblical critic G. A. Smith (though Moody allowed he had enough trouble getting people to believe in any Isaiah to trouble himself with the idea of second Isaiah!). There were Christian Darwinists who turned out to be proto-fundamentalists. For a half century there were stirrings, coalescences, vague and uneasy feelings, callings of conferences— the Niagara Bible conferences being prime. During that half century, premillennialism began to make its way beyond Adventism. Evolutionary thought became ever more given to "natural selection" and thus to arbitrariness and away from design and the possibilities of theism. Biblical criticism did not all turn out to be supportive of faith. Philosophical arguments long nurtured at Princeton began to find wider acceptance elsewhere. A party formed on the soil of evangelicalism. Not until the second decade of the twentieth century was there a name for the party, at the time when the diffuse and randomly aimed tracts called *The Fundamentals* came along. Not all of them are fundamentalist, nor are they all given over to fundamentalist preoccupations.

During World War I and in the years immediately after, the coalescence became a coalition and the parties put away the coffee cups and became a Party. William Jennings Bryan and William Bell Riley, John Roach Straton and J. Gresham Machen, Clarence MacMartney and a host of others—all but J. Frank Norris among the leaders being northern and urban, not southern and rural as the cultural picture holds— found each other and felt the need to make the fight for denominational control.

I argue that the fundamentalists had the same goal as the modernists, but used the opposite tactic. Instead of proclaiming cosmopolitan culture contact around a theology that was at once organic-holistic and cosmic, the fundamentalists were content to give absolutist and satisfying answers within a subcultural cocoon. Invite people into it and satisfy them in it and they have a rationale for denying the competition. In the world of extremes on which fundamentalism nurtured people, ambiguity disappeared. God ruled or Satan did. While fundamentalism may not have done well with the core of personality or church and cultural life—the record is very mixed—it was successful at producing boundaries.

So "wholeness-hunger" was on its agenda, and fundamentalists discerned it with a genius that went beyond the rational. While not eager to be seen as having less than a cosmic outlook or Christology, the fundamentalists in their vision came off as cramped and parochial—but only to outsiders. It matched modernist imperialism, not by encompassing definitions of people in other religions, but by fundamentalist attempts to convert people from other religions, efforts to "do others in." Fundamentalism differed vastly from modernism by holding generally to a world that was not progressive or evolutionary but thereby satisfying the need of many to have a secure point in a turning world, a place where things "stayed put."

We can continue the parallels and contrasts: fundamentalism must have been therapeutic to the people who used it to be away from the winds and acids of modernity. Let outsiders call the sheltered vision "bad faith"; to those who held it, it was simply faith. As for being scientific, literate fundamentalists would not yield on that point. Princeton helped them with a Baconian inductivism which they applied to the scriptural texts. They were "facts" issuing propositionally from the mind of a rational God, addressed to the rational aspect of humanity, and capable of being dissected, analyzed, clarified, and demonstrated as easily as geologists handled rocks and entomologists did fruit flies. What was unscientific about that? Conversely, it was not a critical outlook, favoring as it did pre- or a-critical views of scriptural revelation and, in many cases, creed and dogma. The static and nondevelopmental world view did not trouble itself much with problems of contingency and relativity.

Where was fundamentalism? Along the Niagara at the Bible conferences; in Minneapolis and Tennessee in the Bible institutes; in powerful pulpits in downtown Boston and Toronto; in its intellectual girding, at Princeton seminary and its later dissident offspring; in many a denominational seminary in the conservative camps; on the radio; represented in the independent mission boards; among many lay people of Bryan's stripe; in business community and on red-dirt hilltops of the South alike. Not all fundamentalists were pessimistic because they thought the world was ending soon and everything had to get worse for Jesus to come. There were buoyant optimists among them.

Like two great competitors, the fundamentalists fought about human destiny. Were they less plausible than the Marxist rivals who talked of a messianic future classless society for which there was no more empirical support than for their millennium? As for the more potent American futurism, the progressive outlook, how in the 1930s could people point to progress? Over against these, premillennial views which often turned into what James Barr called "mythopoetic fantasies" of great filiation—dispensational, pretribulational, raptural premillennialism vied with subtle alternatives—seemed to be as well grounded in trends and reality. Out of this impulse grew the then curious pro-Zionism based on allegorical-literal readings of visionary Biblical books, an outlook that made later fundamentalism so relevant to Israel.

As with futures, so with present securities. Over against the higher critics' views of the Bible, vaunted for their science, Princeton and its kith imported Aristotle, Bacon, and Scottish Common Sense Realism to make the claim that it rightfully held to science. And as for pasts, and accounting for origins, the fundamentalists became masters at exploiting empirical gaps and evidential missed points in the intra-evolutionary spats. Fixity and the creation of a completed world, complete with fossils in different strata, seemed as reasonable to the fundamentalist mentality as evolution, since one could not point to missing links and fillers of gaps in transit between species.

There were problems, which opponents spotted at once. The fundamentalist vision was not catholic nor historically accurate when it tried to show that its part was the whole, that it was in continuity with orthodoxy, or that it simply replicated old orthodoxy in a new day. The historian knew that once there had been orthodoxy without or before Aristotle, Bacon, Paley, Scots of the Enlightenment, and that the new arguments for the Bible

35

differed from the "pre-scientific" ones that Luther and Calvin had advocated— and were not they orthodox? Fundamentalism bred an integralist outlook that came apart if any chink fell out of it. Before long there was a generation of overprogrammed fundamentalists' children who had to use parachutes into mainline churches or who landed on the hard soil of reactive secularity. There was something introverted, uncatholic, anticultural about fundamentalism in its attitude toward the arts, learning, and culture that disturbed moderate Protestants who might have shared some of its witness and theology.

This is not the place to enter into a philosophical criticism of fundamentalist rationalism or premillennialism. I have contented myself chiefly with the historical case: once there was not fundamentalism and then there was, and it was a particular product of its time and place, a dedicated address to the modern condition. If this analysis is designed to set the fundamentalist attraction in its historical context and to minimize a crisis by showing that there were other alternatives beyond it and modernism, it is not the time to issue an evangelical call to "my" alternative.

As a relatively innocent bystander beyond or between the parties, I would content myself to say that the historian does not necessarily possess traces and evidences that will settle all historical disputes, and necessarily does not possess satisfying philosophical or theological answers to the eternal questions. This one contents himself by paying homage to the dedication of modernists and fundamentalists who set out to address their own and their contemporaries' "hunger for wholeness." We can go further and say that not all their responses were more implausible than many that pass for wisdom or therapy today. He only takes away from them their preemptive claims for all the truth or the illusion they created that they were the only significant alternatives. If those alternatives are to be explored in the 1980s, some of the intentions and maybe some of the instruments of modernism and fundamentalism are likely to live on. One hopes for more commitment than latter-day civil modernists displayed, and more civility than committed fundamentalists have ordinarily expressed.

ABOUT MARTIN E. MARTY

The third Edmondson Lecturer is Fairfax M. Cone Distinguished Service Professor at the University of Chicago. Dr. Marty received the B.A. degree from Concordia Seminary (1949), the M. Div. degree from Concordia (1952), the S.T.M. degree from Lutheran School of Theology (1954), and the Ph.D. degree in church history from the University of Chicago in 1956.

Dr. Marty was ordained to the Lutheran ministry in 1952 and served as pastor for eleven years. Since 1963 he has taught the history of modern Christianity at the Divinity School of the University of Chicago and has also taught in the university's history department. Concurrently, he has been visiting professor at the Lutheran School of Theology and Union Theological Seminary.

Dr. Marty is the author of some twenty books, the most significant of which are:

The New Shape of American Religion (1959);
A Short History of Christianity (1959);
The Improper Opinion: Mass Media and the Christian Faith (1961);
Second Chance for American Protestants (1963);
Church Unity and Church Mission (1964);
Varieties of Unbelief (1964);
The Search for a Usable Future (1968);
The Modern Schism: Three Paths to the Secular (1969);
Righteous Empire: The Protestant Experience in America (1970; National Book Award);
Protestantism (1972);
The Fire We Can Light: The Role of Religion in a Suddenly Different World (1973);
The Pro and Con Book of Religious America: A Bicentennial Argument (1975);
A Nation of Behavers (1976); and
Religious Awakening and Revolution (1977).

Dr. Marty's current project, "Sacred Journeys," is an illustrated work on 500 years of American religion and is being considered as the basis for a television series.

He has also co-authored and edited ten other books including:

The Religious Press in America (1963) and
What Do We Believe? The Stance of Religion in America (1968).

Dr. Marty is associate editor of *Christian Century*, co-editor of *Church History*, and editor of the newsletter, *Context*. He is past president of the American Society of Church History and president-elect of the American Catholic Historical Association. His contributions to the major international encyclopedias and scholarly and popular journals are too numerous to list. He is an elected fellow of the American Academy of Arts and Sciences, the Society of American Historians, the American Antiquarian Society, and other honorary societies. He serves on numerous boards and is active in the National Humanities Center, the Commission on the Humanities, the Author's Guild, the National Book Critics Circle, and a number of historical associations.

In recognition of his outstanding achievements in his chosen discipline, fourteen colleges and seminaries have conferred on Dr. Marty various honorary degrees—Litt.D., LL.D., D.D., D.Hum., and L.H.D.

In 1952 Dr. Marty married Elsa Schumacher. The Marty family now includes four sons and two foster children.

Publication of this volume of the Edmondson Historical Lectures has been made possible by contributions from Baylor University and the following individuals:

N. J. Bellegie

J. D. Bragg

William R. Carden

Jesse Derrick

Irene C. Hanna

Harry W. Diddie

Colbert C. Held

Robert T. Miller

Louis S. Muldrow

Bruce Neatherlin

Robert L. Reid

Jack M. SoRelle

Rufus B. Spain

PREVIOUS PUBLICATIONS IN THE
CHARLES EDMONDSON HISTORICAL LECTURE SERIES

1. Paul K. Conkin, *American Christianity in Crisis:*
   "Religious Rationalism—God without a Redeemer,"
   "Darwinism—Nature without a Creator." (1978)

2. Walter LaFeber, *Crises in American Foreign Policy: The*
   Third Cold War:
   "The Kissinger Years,"
   "The Carter Years." (1980)